STORIES FROM MRS. ROBINSON'S E-LEARNING ADVENTURE

J.H. KIEREN

BOOKS

Bulk ordering is available for educational, business, or sales
promotional use. For information, please contact the publisher at
www.jnhbooks.com

Library of Congress Control Number: 2021909095
ISBN 978-1-7370821-0-1 (paperback)
ISBN 978-1-7370821-1-8 (e-book)
First Edition 2021

JNH Books
Minnetonka, Minnesota
visit us at www.jnhbooks.com

Dedicated to all of the teachers out there who manage e-learning with such grace and patience.

Especially:
Mrs. Bailey
Mrs. Forsman
Mrs. McIvor
Mrs. Barry
Mr. Anderson
Mrs. Friends
Mrs. Kenealy-Bredice
Mrs. Anderson
Teacher Ashley

It was a pleasure to have you in our home each week!

CONTENTS

INTRODUCTION

After 39 years of teaching kindergarten, Mrs. Robinson had only one year left. The thought of having one year left made Mrs. Robinson both happy and sad. She was sad because she would miss the kids. Mrs. Robinson loved the kids, but she was also tired—

very, very, very tired. Mrs. Robinson was ready for a much-needed break.

She was looking forward to a life of leisure and travel. Mrs. Robinson had many places she longed to visit, like Iceland, Australia, Italy, and Paris. She had dreams of drinking the day away with cup after cup of espresso and saying, "Bonjour" to all who passed her. Then the virus came and changed everything. Poor Mrs. Robinson didn't know what to do or what to expect.

When Mrs. Robinson found out she would be teaching a class online instead of in a classroom, she felt again both happy and sad. She was happy because she would get to be home with her cat, Felix, and her dear husband, Fred, but it was hard for her to think she wouldn't get to be with her students every day. She wouldn't get to give them hugs, and help them with their work and little tasks like tying their shoes. She would miss teaching in a classroom, especially since it was her last year.

Mrs. Robinson decided she would no longer be sad about teaching an online class. To be honest, Mrs. Robinson was not the type of person to stay sad about anything for very long. She always found a way to look on the bright side of things. Mrs. Robinson believed everyone has superpowers and hers are to look up not down, look forward not backward, and to always look at the bright side. It was then and there that Mrs. Robinson decided she was going to make this the best year of e-learning anyone had ever had.*

*Yes, Mrs. Robinson was aware that this was the ONLY year of e-learning that anyone had ever had, but Mrs. Robinson was not one to look at those small details and make them change her outlook on the situation at hand. This would be the best e-learning year anyone had ever had and that was all there was to it.

MRS. ROBINSON'S FIRST DAY

Mrs. Robinson started every morning with a cup of black coffee in her faded "best teacher in the world" mug, which was next to the stained coffee maker she kept on her counter next to the sink. She loved that mug and had dozens of others more or less like it on the shelf above the counter. The mugs made her smile, and so did the coffee. She would drink her coffee, with a side of buttered whole wheat toast and a smear of jam, in her sunroom. There she would sip the coffee, read the paper while petting Felix, and hum to herself. It was a lovely routine and a very good start to her day.

Today it was harder for her to read the paper and pet Felix at the same time because she had the first-day-of-school jitters. She still hummed but it was faster and louder than the soft, gentle, sweet hum with which she greeted every other day.

"It's no use," she said looking at Felix.

Felix purred back to her as if to say, "Is it now?"

"I'm not going to be able to read a thing this morning," Mrs. Robinson continued.

She picked up the paper, only to throw it back down across the round table in front of her. She turned her head and looked out her window as the sun was coming up past the trees across from her house. Her husband, Fred, entered the room and instantly knew what was wrong. Fred was a smart man and had been married to Mrs. Robinson for all 39 years of her teaching career, and he knew first-day-of-school jitters when he saw them.

"You are going to be fine. It's going to be a great

day, darling," he said as he walked over and kissed the top of her head.

"I know, but this year is different, Fred. Today is my *last* first day. I just can't believe it."

"I know, dear. Just enjoy it—and you better believe it because class will be starting soon," he said.

The noise of his words were replaced with the sound of his coffee pouring into a "world's best teacher" mug.

Once Mrs. Robinson was ready for her class, she logged in to her meeting and waited for the students to arrive. And then she heard "blip, blip, blip, blip" as her new students' faces started to dance across the screen.

This was it. This was her class. As the flashes of faces flooded her screen, so did the noise. It was a volume of noise she was not used to. The intensity was enough to make her want to curl up into a ball. How was she ever going to be able to quiet the noise?

"Well, hello, boys and girls," she said with a smile.

Unfortunately for Mrs. Robinson, her warm greeting did nothing. Her soft, gentle voice just got lost in the shrieks and laughs and banging.

She tried a little louder.

"HELLO, boys and girls."

This time the noise amplified, which she thought

was very peculiar. She knew she was going to have to be louder still to top the noise of these kids.

"HELLO, BOYS AND GIRLS!" she screamed. But it was as if she had said nothing at all.

She thought for a minute. She needed something to grab their attention. She needed something to cut through the commotion. Finally, she had it.

She turned, went over to her father's old piano that sat behind her chair, and made herself comfortable at the piano bench. There she sat and did what she would continue to do every morning from then on out: she sang her good-morning song. It went like this:

> *Good morning, everyone*
> *how lucky am I*
> *to be with you today*
> *Good morning, everyone*
> *how lucky am I*
> *it's a bright and shiny new day*
> *Good morning, everyone*
> *together you and I*
> *can conquer anything*
> *Good morning, everyone*
> *I'm so glad you're here*
> *Won't you please take a seat*
> *and have no fear*

4

with love and laughter
together, you and I
can have a
very good
happy
bright day

To her surprise, there was quiet. Terrified of breaking the silence, Mrs. Robinson slowly turned to look at the faces staring at her. The endless squares of images were lined up, and for the first time, Mrs. Robinson could get a good look at her new class.

"Well then," she said.

She moved from the piano and faced her class.

"Good morning, everyone! Boy am I happy to be with you today, here online, on our first day of kindergarten. I'm Mrs. Robinson, your teacher, and I can't wait to meet all of you."

It was as if her words were an invitation to speak, and the children were ever so eager to accept. The noise produced by the small speakers reached a volume that made her instantly cover her ears. The noise was a mixture of laughter, screaming, and talking—coming all at once from every direction.

"HI, MRS. ROBINSON!"

"How does this thing work?"

"I can't see you. Is anyone there? Mom, it doesn't work. MOM!"

"Are we almost done?"

"My big sister is here too. Can you see her? She's in third grade."

"I don't want to do this! I don't want to go to school. You can't make me."

"HI, MRS. ROBINSON! My favorite color is blue."

"Get out of here. No! I am in class. Get out NOW! MOM! Robbie won't get out."

"Mrs. Robinson, can you hear me? I said, MY FAVORITE COLOR IS BLUE, but …"

"What does this thing do?"

"Did someone just say butt!"

"I can't talk right now; I'm helping Susie with her school. Today's her first day of kindergarten."

"Mom, what do I do now?"

"My ears are hurting from all of this noise."

"Why is it so loud? Can everyone be quiet? I can't even hear a thing this lady is saying."

"Oh dear," Mrs. Robinson said to herself.

She moved back to her piano bench again and started to play.

Bonjour, hola, howdy, good day

These are just a few ways to say
Hello … Hello …
Bonjour, hola, howdy, good day
Say it even louder, there's no wrong way
Hello … Hello ….

When Mrs. Robinson stopped singing, she slowly turned to face her audience. The kids were silent once more. Scared to even move an inch for fear of disrupting the silence, she pulled her legs around from the bench and froze. She had to take control of the situation at once or she would lose them again.

"I am going to need everyone to be quiet for a moment. Please do that for me. Just be nice and quiet so everyone can hear."

She stood up and quickly sat in the chair in front of her desk. There was still a ringing of background noise, but no one was talking. As if she knew this could only last so long, Mrs. Robinson kept going.

"This will only work if we are all nice and quiet when I am talking. I need everyone to remain quiet, just while I talk. And I promise when I am done, you will all get a chance to introduce yourselves."

She paused for a moment and then realized she must quickly continue.

"I am Mrs. Robinson, your teacher for the year. I have been teaching kindergarten for 39 years ..."

And before she could finish, a little boy spoke up.

"Wow that means you are, like, really old. You are older than my mom; she is, like, 34, I think. Or maybe, like, 24 or 54 maybe. Mom, how old are you again?"

Mrs. Robinson could see who was talking: the little boy's face took up half her screen. He had light brown hair and wore a blue T-shirt with an orange dinosaur on the front.

"I am going to need everyone to be quiet until I am finished and call on you. As I said, I have been teaching for 39 years and this is my last year, which means it is going to be a really special year. I can already tell from looking at you that this is a really special group of kids."

"Will your hair always look crazy like that?" a little girl asked.

Her face popped up on Mrs. Robinson's screen. Her name was Susie. She had big eyes and brown hair with little curls that sat softly on her shoulders. After she spoke, there was laughter but no one else said a word.

"My hair?" Mrs. Robinson quickly felt the top of her head.

"Will my hair always look this crazy? Does it look

crazy to you? Has someone done something to it? Let me see."

Mrs. Robinson pretended to frantically feel all over her head.

"You know what happened? I let my elves help me with my hair this morning in preparation for our first day, and they might have gone a little overboard."

"Your elves?" Susie asked with a giggle, "You have elves?"

"How else would you expect me to get all of the work a teacher has to do done without helpers? I have teacher elves."

"Can we meet them?"

"What elves?"

"Look at your hair. It's wild."

"You have ELVES?"

"Are they real elves?"

"Did somebody say elves?"

"Quiet everyone. Remember what I said, only one of us can talk at a time, otherwise it hurts everyone's ears.

"This is going to be a marvelous year and don't you worry, you will hear all about my elves at some point. For now, we need to start our day."

And start the day they did. Mrs. Robinson learned a lot of lessons after that first day of e-learning, like where the mute button was. How to get the kids to use the mute button. How to get the kids to use inside voices. Most importantly, she learned to always check herself in the mirror before class because there is no telling what a five-year-old might say.

2

WHERE'S JAKE?

One of the first tasks Mrs. Robinson had to tackle was getting the kids to keep their faces on the screen. It may seem like an easy task, but don't be fooled by the simplicity of tasks when dealing with a large group of five-year-olds. Ask any parent and they will tell you, even the simple task of getting ready in the morning can take hours, and getting the kids to sit still with their face on the screen was just as challenging. For Mrs. Robinson, the task took weeks. And even by the end of the year, not everyone complied, especially Jake.

Mrs. Robinson started working on it that first week of school.

"OK, boys and girls, we are going to talk about the proper way to sit so that everyone can see your lovely faces. Now, take me for example. What if I were to sit like this?"

Mrs. Robinson moved her body over to the right so that only an ear and some hair were showing.

"Or what if I sat like this?"

Mrs. Robinson scooched over to the other side of her chair, which proved harder to do, since she almost fell off it entirely in the process. She caught her balance by holding the desk in front of her. She continued to slouch, and now only the top left side of her head was showing.

"Or what if I taught class like this?"

Mrs. Robinson got out of her chair altogether and walked away, leaving behind an empty chair, only the back of which could be seen on screen. Her voice echoed as she continued to talk from a distance.

"Can you guys see me? Would it be hard for you to understand me if I taught our class like this?"

With that simple question, Mrs. Robinson forgot rule number one: don't ask a question to a group of kindergarteners without first reminding them to raise their hands and not shout out the answer.

"I can't see you but I can hear you."

"How much longer are we going to do this for?"

"She's gone. Now we can have fun!"

"I can see you! Just kidding. I can't even see your crazy hair."

"Mrs. Robinson, I have to go potty."

"Does this mean class is over?"

"Can we be done now?"

"Seriously, Mrs. Robinson, I have to go potty really bad."

"I can't see you, but can you see me?"

"Remember what I said about keeping your mute button on until I call on you."

Mrs. Robinson got back into her chair, and now her entire face made up the screen.

"As you can see, it's a lot harder to pay attention when we don't have everyone in the center of their screen. Look at how I am in the center of my screen. You can see my entire face. You can hear what I am saying and you can see what I am teaching. This is how I need everyone to be in our classes. What I want us to do next is practice the proper way to sit for class."

Mrs. Robinson sat up straight in her chair and waited.

"Mrs. Robinson, can you see me now?"

"Am I doing it?"

"For real, Mrs. Robinson, I really gotta go potty."

"How about now?"

"Like this?"

"Everyone should have their mute buttons on. Remember? But who just said they needed to use the bathroom?"

"I did," said Nate, a small boy with a big smile.

"Yes, Nate, of course you can go to the bathroom."

"OK, I will be right back."

"Yes, that is fine. Now, how is everyone else doing?"

"Good!"

"Great!"

"Good!"

"Good!"

"Good work, Marcus. You guys are all doing so well. Emily, can you move a little to your left? Yes, that's it. Wonderful, everyone. Now, let me see. Do we have everyone? Yes, that looks great. No, just wait, someone has their camera on the ceiling. Who is that? Jake? Jake are you there?"

But Jake was not there. Jake is what Mrs. Robinson would later call a magician because he was always making himself disappear.

"Jake, I am going to need you to come and join the rest of the class. Jake? Are you there, Jake? I would like to see your face."

Mrs. Robinson couldn't possibly wait all day for Jake to come around. Time was of the essence with kindergarteners.

"OK, Jake, when you are ready to come back, please do so. But for now, we are going to move on."

"Hi, Mrs. Robinson" said a little voice.

"I'm sorry, who said that?" Mrs. Robinson asked.

Then she heard "Me, I'm over here," followed by some giggles.

Mrs. Robinson scanned the rows of faces on her screen.

"Can you see me now?" And with that, Jake's face popped up on the screen.

"There you are. Yes, Jake, I see you. It's nice of you to rejoin the class."

"I was here the whole time. I could hear you but I was hiding."

"Yes, we saw that, Jake, but right now is not the

time for games. We have a lot to get through and we must all focus."

Half of Jake's head was on the screen as he held his computer and started making faces into the camera. The class could only see his tongue hanging out of his mouth.

"Jake, I am going to need you to put the camera down and pay attention."

Jake put his device back down. But now the only part of his face you could see was his chin.

"Jake, can you move your body so we can see your whole face?" Mrs. Robinson asked.

Jake moved, and now the only thing you could see was his left ear, some hair, and the wall behind him.

"Jake, we still can't see your face. Can you try that again?"

There was a ruffling sound as Jake moved his camera around and finally it stopped. Jake was in the lower corner of his screen and only his forehead, one eye, and hair were showing.

"Jake, you still don't have it. We want to see your entire face, like this. Look at my screen. See how you can see my entire face, not just part of my face? I want to see your entire face."

There was more rustling as Jake, once again, tried

to reposition his camera. Finally, the camera stopped moving with a bang.

"Jake? Now all we can see is the ceiling. Jake, are you there? Jake, I need you to try again. Jake?" Mrs. Robinson called out to Jake but he never replied, although she could hear giggling and the sound of shuffling paper.

"Jake? Jake? Jake?" Mrs. Robinson continued to call out.

After a couple of minutes she gave up.

"Jake, can you at least mute your mic?"

The shuffling noise stopped, but the sound of footsteps and giggling remained.

Jake leaned over the camera exposing his entire face for the class to see. His bangs hung down in front of his eyes.

"Sure," he said.

With a satisfied look on his face, Jake muted his microphone. It was the first time Mrs. Robinson had seen his face all day. At least he showed his face and muted his microphone, Mrs. Robinson thought to herself. That might just be all she was going to get out of Jake. She smiled and continued with her lesson.

3

INTERRUPTING SUSIE

Sometimes, no matter how hard Mrs. Robinson tried, things didn't go as planned, as can be expected with a large group of kindergarteners. One of the things Mrs. Robinson constantly struggled with was getting the kids to take turns talking. This was especially difficult when there was a little

Susie in the class.

Susie was adorable; there were no other words to describe her. She had big brown eyes, soft brown curls and a smile that stretched from one ear to the other. She was also one of the oldest kids in the class. But regardless of her age, she was naturally wise beyond her years. Susie was also an only child and was used to having all eyes on her.

Yes, Susie was a very special little girl, but sometimes the qualities that made Susie special didn't always help her in class.

"OK, class, today we are going to learn about the letter L," Mrs. Robinson said while standing.

"I already know about the letter L, Mrs. Robinson," Susie said.

Mrs. Robinson looked at her screen. Susie's face took up half of it. She watched as Susie wiggled her shoulders and body up higher, eager to share her knowledge with the class.

"That's wonderful, Susie, but I still want you to be patient and follow along. There may be some things we discuss that you don't know."

"No, I don't think so," said Susie.

"Remember to raise your hand if you have something to say." Mrs. Robinson replied.

Susie raised her hand.

"Yes, Susie?"

"What should I do if I already know about the letter L?" Susie asked.

"Just listen quietly because there may be others in the class who are still learning. We want to make sure everyone can hear and learn."

Susie raised her hand again.

"Yes, Susie?"

"Like starts with the letter L and so does learn."

"Yes, they do start with the letter L. We are going to move on now and start our lesson."

"Lesson also starts with the letter L. See, I told you I know all about the letter L." Susie's voice echoed through the speakers.

"I know the letter L too."

"Like also starts with L."

"Loolaaloolalo also starts with L."

"I love the letter L. Get it? Love starts with the letter L. I *love* the letter L. Get it?"

"Please mute your microphones, everyone. Susie, please keep your computer on mute from here on out so I can get on with the lesson. Let's stay quiet, everyone, so everyone can hear me."

Susie raised her hand again.

"Susie, I am going to have you wait a minute so I can get started."

"It's just really quick, Mrs. Robinson. I also know that like starts with L. Someone said that and I wanted you to know I had said it first."

"Yes, thank you, Susie."

Mrs. Robinson pushed her hair away from her face as she moved closer to the whiteboard. She grabbed her black marker and held it in a writing position. She looked back at the camera.

"As we already discussed, the letter of the day is L. And as some of you already pointed out, there are a lot of words that begin with L. Now, please grab something to write with and on."

Mrs. Robinson put her face closer to the screen.

"Done."

"I'm ready."

"What were we gonna get?"

"My mom won't help me and I don't know where it is, Mrs. Robinson."

"Got it."

"Now we are going to work on writing our letters."

"Mrs. Robinson, I already know how to write my letters. I can even write my name." Susie said.

"Yes, Susie, we talked about that. That's fine but I still want you to practice your writing, even if you already know how."

"Since I know my letters already, can I just draw?" Susie asked.

"No, Susie, you can't. I still want you to write your letters. I want everyone to practice. We are going to write the letter L."

"I can help you teach, Mrs. Robinson. I already know my letters. All of them," Susie continued.

"Yes, Susie we have established that. I need you to just stay on mute and practice with everyone else.

"Are we going to write the little L or the big L?"

"We are going to practice both."

"Oh good, 'cause I know how to write them both," Susie smiled.

"Yes, OK, now mute your microphone, Susie. Thank you so much."

"You're welcome, Mrs. Robinson. But, Mrs. Robinson, one more thing …"

4

MARCUS, PLUS ONE

J ust as there are kids that don't want to go to school, there are also kids that do not want to go to school online. Marcus was one of those kids.

It was not that he didn't like Mrs. Robinson, because he did: he thought she was very nice and silly.

He also enjoyed the songs she sang and the way her voice sounded when she sang them. It wasn't that he didn't want to learn. Marcus was very curious and loved learning new things. It was not that he didn't like the kids. In fact, he loved the kids, especially Logan, who always showed the class the new toys he would get from his grandparents. You could say he loved the kids so much it made him feel shy.

The only way Marcus was going to join his class online was if his mother joined too. Luckily, Marcus's mother was very patient, much like Mrs. Robinson. Marcus's mother only meant to join him on a few of his classes, but one thing led to another and before she knew it, she had become a regular. Even when Mrs. Robinson and the class couldn't see her, she was there.

Most days Marcus and his mother observed the class from the shadows. To the class, it looked as if no one was there. But Marcus was there. He was there and he was listening. He was even watching. That's the thing with online learning: you can find ways to watch the class without the class watching you.

"Marcus? Are you there, Marcus? I am taking attendance and I need to know if you are with us, Marcus," Mrs. Robinson said.

Mrs. Robinson's words were met with silence.

Marcus's camera showed an empty chair and an empty bed behind it.

"Marcus?" Mrs. Robinson asked again.

"Hi. Yes, he is here. Sorry, this is Marcus's mom."

Half of Marcus's mom's disheveled face appeared on screen.

"Marcus is here; he's listening. He doesn't want to come onscreen still, but he is here."

"OK, Marcus!" Mrs. Robinson shouted through the computer. "Marcus, we would love for you to join us on our call. I know everyone would love to see you. So when you are ready to join us, please do so."

"Did you hear that, Marcus? Are you ready to join? Come on, it will be just fine."

Marcus's mother motioned for him to come toward her.

"It will be fun. They are going to have story time soon. Come on, Marcus. Please."

Marcus didn't budge.

"Come over here. Come."

Marcus's mom's words, face, and hand signals became more aggressive.

She turned to looked back at the camera, "I'm sorry. He just won't come."

"That is OK. He will come when he is ready,"

Mrs. Robinson assured her. "Let's move on. Violet? Yes, I saw Violet."

"Marcus, please just come join this meeting. I don't want to keep asking you. Your class wants to see you."

Marcus's mom's words echoed through the meeting. She had forgotten to mute her microphone. This was not the first time it happened. In fact, it happened all the time.

"Hello. Sorry! We can still hear you. Would you please mute your mic."

"Marcus, come on! Get on your meeting. Please, just for a little while."

"I'm sorry, we can hear you Marcus's mom. Marcus? Your mic is on."

"Oh no!" Marcus's mom's face turned bright red.

Her face quickly disappeared, and all the class could see was a huge hand, as Marcus's mom reached to mute her microphone.

"As I said, not a big deal. Marcus can join us when he's ready," Mrs. Robinson continued.

"Last but not least, Jake and Susie. Yes, I've seen both of you. It looks as though we are all here today. Now, let's move on. Today we will be talking about the letter R and all of the interesting things that start with the letter R."

While Mrs. Robinson grabbed her black marker, Marcus's mom convinced her son to rejoin the class.

"Before we get started, we are going to practice writing the letter R because writing our letters properly is the first step in writing and reading. I want everyone to grab something to write on and with. I will give you 10 seconds to find your things."

Mrs. Robinson began to sing.

ONE little ant went strolling by
TWO little spiders came and said hi
THREE little birds went chirp, chirp, chirp
and FOUR big frogs went burp, burp, burp
FIVE beautiful butterflies flapped their wings
while SIX hummingbirds began to sing
SEVEN woodpeckers pecked at the tree
and a fly left the spiderweb, finally free
EIGHT noisy geese went flying by
while on the sidewalk NINE beetles lie
TEN little children watched them all
suddenly no longer feeling so small

When she finished her song, she examined her screen.

Mrs. Robinson noticed Marcus, who was now sitting on his mother's lap. His mother had a tight grip on him with both her arms wrapped around his body. As Mrs. Robinson looked closer, she could see there was a struggle. Mrs. Robinson had a decision to make: did she say something or ignore it?

She decided to ignore it.

"Let's begin with the big R, shall we? To write the big R, we start with a straight line."

Mrs. Robinson began writing on her whiteboard.

"What's wrong with Marcus?" Susie interrupted.

Mrs. Robinson turned around scanning all the small squares for Marcus. He was still in his mother's lap, but red in the face. Tears streamed down his cheeks and his arms were violently flailing about.

"Oh dear," Mrs. Robinson's words slipped out of her mouth.

Marcus's computer was on mute but you could see the intensity and volume of his words.

"Marcus, is everything OK?"

Mrs. Robinson couldn't help herself. Everyone saw it, and at this point there was no pretending everything was all right because clearly everything was not all right. In fact, it looked as though poor Marcus was being tortured.

Marcus's mom quickly unmuted the microphone to reassure Mrs. Robinson that Marcus was fine. But unmuting his microphone proved to be a big mistake.

"I DON'T WANT TO! LET GO OF ME!" Marcus wailed.

"Yes, Mrs. Robinson, we are fine. Marcus is just having a hard time."

You could barely make out her words over the screams and hysterics coming out of Marcus.

"Why don't you and Marcus take a little break. Come back and join us when he is feeling better. How does that sound?"

Marcus's mom hesitated. Marcus was sliding down the side of her body as she struggled to keep him in her lap. She tried to hold on to him but finally her arms loosened and he tumbled to the floor with a bang. Now all you could see was the top of his head, which was still tilted back, his eyes shut tight. His forehead was bright red and his hair was sticking straight up as if he had slept with it wet.

Marcus's mom didn't want to give up so easily, but when she looked at Mrs. Robinson's concerned face, she knew what she needed to do.

"Yes, we are going to take a little break. I don't know what is wrong with him."

That was a lie. She knew what was wrong with him. Everyone knew what was wrong with him. Marcus did not want to be in class. Marcus had other things he wanted to do and e-learning was not one of them.

"We will just be a couple of minutes."

"No rush. We will be here. Take all the time you need," Mrs. Robinson assured her.

"It should only be a couple of minutes," Marcus's mom promised and abruptly left the meeting.

Mrs. Robinson gathered her thoughts. She looked at the stunned faces staring back at her.

"Well then, where were we?"

"We were writing the letter R," answered Susie.

"Yes, the letter R," Mrs. Robinson continued.

Mrs. Robinson continued her lesson on the letter R. They wrote it, sounded it out, and then listed words that begin with it. It had been a successful lesson: the kids learned what they needed to. But Mrs. Robinson couldn't stop thinking of Marcus.

As Mrs. Robinson was wrapping up her lesson, a new image popped up on the screen. It took only a second for Mrs. Robinson to recognize the half of face in front of her.

"Marcus! I am so glad you were able to join us," Mrs. Robinson cheered.

"Yes, we are here," Marcus's mom said from the bottom corner of his screen.

Marcus was no longer crying, his face was no

longer red, and his hair was back in place. He was not smiling but he was content. He had one arm around his mom's head, as she knelt down next to his chair. Marcus had finally agreed to join Mrs. Robinson's meeting with only seconds left—but only with his mom by his side.

5

VIOLET'S LITTLE CUT

I t only took a couple of weeks for the kids to feel comfortable doing their activities independently with Mrs. Robinson guiding them each step of the way. The children used a variety of materials, from glue and scissors to markers and crayons. Mrs. Robinson loved how everyone followed along to her instructions. Mrs. Robinson also appreciated the fact that her home was always clean and tidy and she could watch from afar as the kids went to work.

Neat and tidy were not words used to describe Violet's workspace, although her mother tried hard to keep it that way. Every morning, Violet would sit down to a clean, orderly desk. By the afternoon, you couldn't see the desk or floor that surrounded it. Paper cuttings, pencils, colored pencils, markers, whiteboard markers, food scraps, empty bowls, toys, dolls, and whatever else she touched were scattered about.

It got to be so bad that her mother quit cleaning the room. Her mother didn't see the point in it. She also hoped her rebellion would teach her daughter a lesson in cleaning up after oneself.

Violet quickly grew accustomed to her workspace being a mess. When she needed something, she would just scream for her mother. It worked every time. Her mother didn't have a job, so what else did she have to do?

"MOM! Where is the paper with the baby animals on it?" Violet screamed.

Her mother put down the heavy, white basket of clean clothes she had carried up from the laundry room. She left it in the hallway and burst through the door to Violet's workroom.

"Is your computer muted?" her mother asked.

"What?" Violet answered annoyed.

Violet didn't understand why it mattered if her computer was muted. She didn't ask her how to mute her computer; she wanted the piece of paper the teacher asked her to get—the one with the baby animals.

Violet's mother rushed over to the computer and peeked around the front of it, making sure she was not on camera. It was in fact muted.

"Violet, I have no idea where the paper with baby animals is. You had all of your worksheets for class. Where did you put it? This is why you need to clean up after yourself. You are never going to be able to find anything in here if you don't put things away when you are done with them."

"But that's what you do, Mom."

"What do you mean, that's what I do?" Violet's mom asked, as the blood rushed to her already hot and red face.

"You do the cleaning," Violet said, her big hazel eyes looking up at her mother innocently.

"I do, don't I? I do all the cleaning." Violet's mom looked down at herself.

She was wearing the same yoga pants and sweatshirt she had worn for the last three days. Her hair was pulled up in the same messy bun with strands of it falling in front of her face. She had a pile of laundry waiting to be folded in the hall. She looked around and saw at least three empty bowls with crumbs of the snacks she had brought to Violet. She looked down at the floor and realized she had swept and cleaned that floor more times in the last month than she could count. She did do all the cleaning, but it had to stop. She was not going to clean that room again.

Violet's mom quickly rummaged through the piles of paper on Violet's desk. When she couldn't find anything that resembled what she needed, she moved to the floor—on her hands and knees. The one she needed was nowhere to be seen. Then she grabbed a piece of paper wedged under the table leg.

"Is this what Mrs. Robinson asked for?"

"YES! Mom, that's it! You found it!"

Violet could sense something was wrong with her mother. There was no excitement coming from her in finding the lost paper. Why was there no excitement? Didn't she enjoy helping her find things? Violet wondered.

"I love you, Mommy." Violet said.

She wrapped her arms around her mother's head before her mother had a chance to get up.

"I love you too, but this room needs to get cleaned

and you need to clean it. After school today, you aren't going anywhere until this room is cleaned. And I need you to start finding your own things. You shouldn't have to holler for me every time you need something."

"OK, Mommy," Violet said.

Her mother couldn't help but kiss the top of Violet's head. She then left, closing the door on her way out.

"Did everyone find the worksheet with the baby animals on it?" Mrs. Robinson asked.

Violet lifted up her worksheet and put it in front of the camera for Mrs. Robinson to see.

"Wonderful. It looks like most of us have found the worksheet. Now we are also going to need a pair of scissors and some glue. I will count to 10 and I want everyone to hurry and find your scissors and glue."

Mrs. Robinson started singing her counting song:

ONE little ant went strolling by
TWO little spiders came and said hi …

Violet put both hands down on the table and lifted her bottom off her chair. She almost screamed out for her mom but stopped herself. Her mother's words were still with her: "You don't need to holler for me every time you need something."

Surely, asking for help again would not mean she was doing it every time; she would simply be doing it *one* more time. Violet looked around. The scissors and glue were definitely not right in front of her.

Mrs. Robinson was still singing.

FIVE beautiful butterflies flapped their wings
while SIX hummingbirds began to sing …

She was already on six hummingbirds, how could that be? Violet thought to herself. And with an urgency she didn't know existed, she sprang to action.

"Scissors. Glue," she said quietly to herself.

She flung the papers on her desk in every which direction. She turned around and looked on the floor around her chair. Since she couldn't see the actual floor, she started kicking her feet, and the papers, markers, toys, and pencils scattered about. She ran across her room to the bookshelf. The shelves were not only covered with books but also jars and tins with all sorts of crafting and art materials.

Violet touched each item she looked at. When the scissors and glue weren't there, she moved over to the pile of stuff on the floor in front of her dollhouse. She threw paper after paper about until finally she spotted something pink out of the corner of her eye.

"Scissors!"

She grabbed the scissors and then went back to the bookshelf, remembering that her mother kept glue in the silver tin.

"Glue!"

Violet ran back to her seat and held the scissors and glue up to the screen for Mrs. Robinson and the rest of the class to see. Mrs. Robinson was already cutting.

"You should just be cutting out the pictures of the baby animals. Leave the mommy animals alone, since we will be gluing the baby animals in the boxes next to their mommies," Mrs. Robinson instructed.

Violet started cutting. First she cut nice and slowly, making sure to stay on the dotted line. She held the scissors tighter and brought the paper closer to her face as she rounded the corner of the baby giraffe. Her head was low and her hair hung in front of her face.

She continued to cut, looking down at the paper in her hand, when she noticed pieces of fur falling. Fur? Violet was confused. She stopped cutting and realized it was not fur. It was something else. What could it be? Her hair continued to hang down in front of her and without thinking she pulled a strand back and tucked it behind her ear.

The simple act of touching her hair made her

realize what was spread out across the desk in front of her. It was not fur; it was hair. Her hair. Violet had cut her own hair. Oh no! She looked around to see if anyone had seen her. Wait, no one was in the room. She was alone. Silly Violet, she thought. Then she looked on the screen to see if anyone in class had seen her. They were still cutting out the baby animals— even Mrs. Robinson.

Violet grabbed her hair out from behind her ear and pulled it in front of her face. There it was, on the left side, a short piece of hair not matching the rest of her hair. She giggled a little. She looked down at the scissors. She giggled some more. She looked around again. She looked at the screen.

Then she grabbed the strand of hair on the right side of her face and she cut. She thought at the very least her hair should match. She watched as the pieces of brown hair fell onto her lap and desk. She giggled again.

She liked the way the hair felt when she cut it. It was a different feeling from when she cut paper. There was a smoothness to it, an ease. She put her chin to her chest and tried to examine her hair by letting it fall in front of her face.

Although she couldn't see herself, she felt like she looked very good. She grabbed a chunk of hair off her right shoulder and gripped it in one hand. She cut again. This time the scissors didn't cut as smoothly. The hair was too thick, so she had to take several cuts to break through it.

She was having so much fun cutting that she didn't hear the class talking about her.

"Mrs. Robinson, there is someone cutting her hair."

"Mrs. Robinson, she's cutting her hair."

"Mrs. Robinson, do you see that girl?"

"She's really doing it. She is cutting her hair."

"I think her name is Violet."

"Her name is Violet. I know it is."

"Do you see her? She is cutting her hair."

"Can I cut my hair?"

Violet looked up at her screen. She lowered the scissors and sat quietly. She thought maybe they were talking about someone else.

"You can't cut your hair, Violet. That is not what scissors are for."

"I didn't cut my hair," Violet replied.

"Violet, we saw you cutting your hair."

"No, you see, *that* was an accident."

"Violet? Is your mom or dad there with you?" Mrs. Robinson asked.

"No, my mom said I need to do it myself."

"Yes, that is right, but I don't think she would want you cutting your hair."

"I didn't cut my hair. It was an accident. And it actually is what scissors are for because my haircutter always uses scissors to cut my hair."

"Violet, I think you should go get your mom and show her what happened."

"No, thank you. That's all right."

"Violet, please go get your mother."

Violet had found her face on the screen and examined her new haircut.

"Fine, I will. But first I have to trim the other side. It's uneven."

6

NAKED NATE

Nate was a curious little boy. He loved to play with all kinds of things, like blocks, cars, books, dolls, paint, clay, ribbons, even his food. It didn't matter what was in front of him, Nate would find a way to turn it into a game or toy.

Nate's playful nature did have its downside though, usually where his clothing was concerned.

"For our next activity, I need everyone to get out a piece of paper; it can be any color paper. If you have construction paper, that is even better. We are going to work on a heart project. Any color will do, but if you have a preference grab whatever color you want your heart to be."

Mrs. Robinson checked her screen closely to make sure everyone was following her instructions.

"I will also need you to grab a pencil, scissors, and something to color or decorate your heart with. It can be markers, colored pencils, crayons, stickers, anything you like."

The kids scrambled to find their supplies. Mrs. Robinson watched and realized this might go on for days.

"I am going to give everyone 30 seconds to find their things."

Mrs. Robinson started singing.

ONE little ant went strolling by
TWO little spiders came and said hi ...

The kids began frantically looking for their things.

Some shouted at their mothers. Some shouted at their fathers. While some shouted just to shout. Many jumped out of their chairs and ran around as if their feet were on fire. Some sat in their chairs and barely moved at all, while others continued to doodle and play, having no clue Mrs. Robinson just gave them a task to complete.

Nate's mother kept everything within his arm's reach. He didn't even need to leave his seat to get what Mrs. Robinson asked for. He had stacks of paper, small tins of markers, crayons, colored pencils, regular pencils—anything he may need throughout his day was accounted for. All Nate had to do was simply grab his supplies and wait, but that was not what Nate chose to do.

Nate decided for this assignment he would like to use watercolors. He looked over at the wooden book-shelves across the room. He could see the art supplies in a clear bin his mother kept neatly organized on one of the shelves. Yes, watercolors sounded like a lot more fun than markers or crayons.

First, Nate looked around to make sure no one had heard his thoughts. Luckily for Nate, his mother was too busy with his older sister's work to notice what he was about to do. He quietly got up and took the container of art supplies off the shelf. He rummaged through it to find the small tray of watercolors.

"Yes," Nate cheered silently to himself.

He grabbed two small paintbrushes and went back to his table.

"It looks like we are all ready. So let's begin," Mrs. Robinson announced.

Mrs. Robinson explained how to cut the paper into a heart and how to decorate it.

Once Nate had the paper heart cut out, he set it down on the table in front of him. He grabbed the watercolor tin and opened it to reveal two even rows of vibrant colors. He tapped his brush into the red color but nothing happened.

Water! Nate realized he needed water. Luckily, Nate's mother kept a glass of water on the table. A nice full glass of water, just waiting for a paintbrush to be dipped into it.

Nate dipped his paintbrush into the water, then into the red and smeared the paint across the middle of his heart. He loved the way the water pooled on his paper. He continued to move it around. He wasn't sure what he was painting but he didn't care.

He needed more color, so he dipped the brush back into the water, then into the red paint and quickly brought it back to the paper. He took the brush off the paper and held it while looking at what he had done. As the brush hung in the air, water began dripping from it. Soon there were puddles on the table. Nate didn't notice the puddles but decided the outer edge of his heart needed more paint.

Once his brush met the paper heart again, he rested his elbow on the table. Something wasn't right. Nate's elbow felt wet. He lifted his elbow from the table and noticed the puddles and the water spots on his shirt. He brought his brush closer to his body while he inspected his shirt. Water from his brush dripped onto the bottom of his shirt where his shirt rested on his pants.

Nate looked around. He dropped the paintbrush back into his water glass. Water splashed up and out as the brush landed. Nate looked around again. His mom was still in the other room helping his sister. He could hear them talking. He looked down at his shirt. He inspected his right shirtsleeve. He scrunched the wet part of his sleeve into a ball so the wetness wouldn't touch his skin.

He looked at his screen. Mrs. Robinson was working on her heart. She had the camera pointed down so the kids could watch her progress. She was talking, giving tips and instruction, but Nate heard none of it. He couldn't take his mind off his wet shirt. There was only one thing for him to do.

First he took his arm out of his right sleeve. The shirt was up around his shoulder as his bare arm hung to his side. He could still feel the wet shirt on his stomach. Next, he lifted the whole shirt off. A smile came over his face. He looked around again. No one was watching him. He dropped his shirt to the floor on the left side of his chair.

"Much better," he whispered to himself.

Nate picked up his paintbrush and swooshed it in the orange paint. Once it was completely covered, he threw the brush down on his cut-out heart and mixed the orange with the red. He dipped the brush again and swooshed it around, watching the orange dissolve into the water.

He put the wet brush into the green, slathering it until you could no longer see the black of the brush. He brought it to the heart and began to spread it around. He lifted his brush into the water again. This time when he swooshed it around the sound of the water made him have to go to the bathroom.

Nate looked at his screen and Mrs. Robinson was still working. He pushed his chair back to stand but then looked down. Orange and green paint drops were splattered across the lap of his pants. He rubbed them.

He rubbed them some more, but it only made them worse. He got up and went to the bathroom.

He shut the door. He clicked the lock. He stared at the lock. His mother had always told him never to lock the door, but he felt it was something that needed to be done. He took off his pants and rolled them into a ball and put them in the corner of the room, where the bathtub met the wall.

When Nate was done going to the bathroom, he turned the knob as slowly as he could. He didn't want to make any noise. He took one tiny step out and looked both ways. There was no sign of his mother. He then ran on his tiptoes back into his room. He could hear Mrs. Robinson talking.

"The hearts look wonderful, everyone. You should be so proud of yourselves."

Nate sat back down in his chair and pulled his heart up off the table. He held the heart in front of his camera so Mrs. Robinson could see he had completed the assignment. Although Nate's heart was far from being finished, it did have paint smeared on it, so he felt confident he'd done well.

"You are all going to want to show these to your parents. You should be very proud. I am sure your parents will want to hang these on the refrigerator. They are so good."

"My mom says she doesn't want anything on the refrigerator because she just cleaned it," Susie said.

"Yes, and that's OK; I am sure she will find another spot for it," Mrs. Robinson assured her.

"No, I don't think so. I heard her tell my Aunt Jen that we have enough art work to last a whole lifetime," Susie answered.

"You know, Susie, maybe there is someone else you would like to give your heart to. I am sure your aunts and uncles and grandparents and even your neighbors would love your artwork."

"I don't think so," Susie answered.

"And that's OK. For right now, let's just put your hearts in a safe place, and you can figure out what to do with them later."

Nate stood up, leaned forward, and set his heart on the table behind his computer.

"Oh no!" Mrs. Robinson hollered.

Nate quickly sat back down to see what was the matter with Mrs. Robinson.

"Nate, is that you?" she asked.

Nate looked around. Was she talking to him? Nate put his face up to the camera.

"Nate! What happened to your clothes?" Mrs. Robinson asked.

"They got wet. They also got paint on them," Nate answered.

Nate looked down at his naked body covered only with his light blue underwear and laughed. The truth was Nate preferred not to have clothes on. He was much more comfortable this way. He didn't see what the big deal was.

"I have clothes on. See?"

Nate stood up so Mrs. Robinson could see his underwear.

"Nate, you need to go and put your clothes back on, please," Mrs. Robinson instructed.

The room filled with laughter.

"Everyone needs to keep their microphones muted, please," Mrs. Robinson insisted.

No one listened and the laughter only grew stronger and louder.

"Nate, did you hear me? I need you to go put clothes on this minute."

"He's naked!"

"I can see your underwear!"

"I can't believe he is actually naked."

The laughter and voices covered Mrs. Robinson's request, and Nate realized he had the attention of the whole class.

He picked up his paintbrush, dipped it into the

blue paint and began to paint his chest. It was wet and gooey but unlike wearing a wet shirt, he didn't mind. The class erupted in hysterics. Nate smiled.

"Nate! I need you to put the paintbrush down and get some clothes on," Mrs. Robinson shouted.

Nate stood up and did a little dance in his underwear, laughing the whole time. Then he dipped his brush back in the blue paint to continue to paint his body. It was then, that his mother's voice stopped him in his tracks and he dropped the brush.

"Nate! What on earth! What are you doing?" his mother shrieked.

"Painting!" Nate answered.

"Are you in a meeting?" His mother ran over to his computer to see if it was on.

"Nate! What in the world! You are in class. You can't be naked in class."

"I'm not naked, I have my underwear on and I was just about to paint on a shirt—I mean, put on a shirt," he giggled.

"Painting your body does not count as clothes. Come on. Right now," she said while grabbing his arm.

She put her face in front of the camera.

"I am so sorry, Mrs. Robinson."

"It is not a big deal. He can rejoin the class once he's dressed." Mrs. Robinson said.

"Yes, of course. He will be right back. Again, I am so sorry. This will not happen again."

Nate's camera went black.

Mrs. Robinson giggled to herself, for she knew better.

7

SOPHIA'S BEST FRIEND

Sophia had always wanted a dog. In fact, she had been begging her parents for one ever since she knew they existed. She wanted a small one, but not too small. Just small enough to fit in her bed but big enough to wrap her whole body around. She wanted it to be brown and black with soft ears and kind eyes. Most of all, she wanted it to be her best friend.

Her parents, on the other hand, did not want a dog. They made sure to tell her they would not be getting one every chance they got. They believed in setting realistic expectations. They thought if they told her up front, she would quit asking. The problem was Sophia never quit asking. In fact, the more they told her they would never get one, the more she wanted one.

Although Sophia's parents had solid arguments, none of them seemed to stick.

"We aren't home enough to get a dog," they would tell her.

"Then let's stay home more. I don't need to go anywhere," Sophia would respond.

"Dogs are a lot of work," they would add.

"I will do all the work. You won't even know it's here," Sophia would plead.

"But we will know it's here because it will leave hair all over the house."

"I will clean up every hair."

"You don't even clean up your own hair. In fact, you don't even comb your own hair."

"Well, then I will start," Sophia insisted.

Their arguments went around like this until

Sophia would finally drop it. That is, until the next time she got reminded of the one thing missing in her life.

Then it happened. Quarantine. Suddenly, everywhere they went they saw puppies. They would see them on their nightly family walks. They would see them hanging out the window of the cars they passed on the street. They would see them at the park, eager to give a sniff in exchange for a belly rub. Even their friends and neighbors were getting them. They were surrounded by puppies. Every time they saw one, Sophia would start up on her parents again. Eventually it wore them down until finally they could no longer say no.

On a cool Saturday morning, Sophia got the puppy she had always dreamed of. Her name was Sadie. She was small, fluffy, curious, friendly, and the cutest thing Sophia had ever seen. She had light brown fur, big eyes, floppy ears, and gentle paws. Most importantly, she was indeed Sophia's best friend. She went everywhere with Sophia, and that is where our problem begins.

"Sophia, we have talked about this before. We all love Sadie but no dogs allowed during class," her mom whispered so the rest of the class couldn't hear.

"No, it's OK, Mom, because she is just going to lie at my feet."

Sophia looked up at her mom with desperation in her eyes. Her mom hated this look. It was very hard to say no when Sophia looked at her like this. She also didn't want to argue with her daughter when she was in the middle of her class.

"She must stay on the floor at your feet the whole time. And if she becomes a distraction, she has to leave," her mom whispered from the doorway.

"Promise!" Sophia shrieked.

"I want everyone to take out their writing journals," Mrs. Robinson instructed.

Sophia went across the room to the purple wired bin where she kept all of her school supplies.

"Writing journal, writing journal, writing journal," she murmured to herself as she flipped through all of her workbooks and worksheets.

"There you are." Sophia grabbed the packet.

When Sophia got back to her desk, Sadie was sitting in her chair pawing at her. Sophia laughed at the sight.

"What do you think you are doing up there?" Sophia said.

"I want everyone to turn to the next blank page in

their journal. Today we are going to write about our favorite animal."

"Our favorite animal! Did you hear that, Sadie? I get to write about you today because you know you are my favorite animal—no question about that."

Sophia grabbed Sadie with her free hand and sat down, plopping Sadie in her lap. She glanced at the door to make sure her mother wasn't around. She held Sadie tight, inhaling her new-puppy smell.

"I don't think it would hurt if you joined me for my class just this one time."

"We are going to begin by writing, 'I like,' and then write your favorite animal. It could be a dog or cat. Maybe it's a lion or bear. Anything you like."

Sophia scooched Sadie over to her left side and grabbed her pencil to begin writing. Sadie watched as Sophia wrote the letter I.

The writing excited Sadie. She tried to get out of Sophia's grip. Once she had a little wiggle room, she put both front paws up on Sophia's desk. She opened her mouth and lunged for Sophia's pencil as Sophia was writing the word "like."

The activity caught Mrs. Robinson's attention.

"Sophia, is that a dog on your screen?" Mrs. Robinson asked.

Sophia quickly unmuted her microphone to respond.

"No, there is no dog on my screen, you are on my screen."

"I didn't mean on your actual screen, dear; I meant is there a dog with you?"

"Yes, this is Sadie. Can you say 'hi,' Sadie? Say 'hi,'" Sophia squeaked.

"She is my new puppy. She is also my favorite animal," Sophia added.

"Wow, you got a new puppy. How exciting! That's wonderful, Sophia, but I am going to need you to put her down so you can work in your journal. OK, dear?"

"Yes, of course. Let me just set her down."

Sophia grabbed Sadie with both hands and put her on the ground next to her chair. Sadie instantly started to whine. Then, she started to scratch at Sophia's chair. After the scratching, she jumped up, putting her two front paws onto Sophia's lap.

"No, Sadie, down; you can't come up here. You heard Mrs. Robinson: no dogs allowed."

"Sophia, dear, would you please mute your microphone?" Mrs. Robinson asked.

Sophia muted her microphone without saying a word. She looked back down at Sadie, while Mrs. Robinson continued with her lesson.

"Where were we? Everyone should have written down 'I like' and then named your favorite animal. On the next line, I want you to write 'I see' and then name the animal again. So if you said 'dog,' you should write 'I see a dog.' Like this."

Mrs. Robinson turned to her whiteboard and began writing her sentence. Sadie continued to cry for Sophia.

Sophia didn't mean to disobey her mother and Mrs. Robinson again. The problem was Sadie wanted her and Sophia wanted Sadie. Sophia checked to make sure Mrs. Robinson wasn't watching then bent down and grabbed Sadie.

"Shh … You have got to be quiet if I am going to hold you," Sophia instructed.

Sadie nuzzled right into her chest and Sophia was the happiest girl in the world.

"How is it going, everyone? How are your sentences coming along?"

Mrs. Robinson turned to see her class. Mrs. Robinson's voice caught Sadie's attention and in a split second, she was pawing at the computer. All Mrs. Robinson could see was Sadie's big, black nose.

"What is that on your screen, Sophia?" Mrs. Robinson asked.

Sophia quickly yanked Sadie away from the computer.

"Sorry, Mrs. Robinson. Sadie needed me again."

"Sophia, it seems Sadie, although adorable, is becoming too much of a distraction for our class."

"It won't happen again, Mrs. Robinson."

Sophia kissed Sadie on the side of her face and then placed her back down on the ground.

"Thank you."

"Now I want everyone to show me your sentences. When you are done writing, hold your paper up to the screen so I can see everyone's work."

Sophia quickly grabbed her pencil and started writing her sentences.

I like dog.

I see dog.

While she was writing, Sadie whined at her feet.

"Quiet now. Remember I am in class. You need to be quiet," Sophia said.

"I want to see everyone's sentences before we move on," Mrs. Robinson instructed.

Sophia picked up her paper to show Mrs. Robinson. As she was holding the paper in her hand, Sadie jumped up and pawed her.

"Down, Sadie, down."

Sophia brought her hands down to her lap to stop

Sadie from jumping up. Her journal fell to the floor. Sadie pulled her legs off of Sophia and went for the paper. Sophia hadn't noticed it fall.

"Sophia, can you show me the sentences in your journal, please?" said Mrs. Robinson.

Sophia unmuted her mic.

"Of course, it's right here," Sophia said.

Sophia panicked. It was not right there. In fact, her journal was not right anywhere. She frantically looked all over her desk with both her eyes and hands.

"It's got to be here somewhere. I just did it. Hold on, just one minute," Sophia continued.

"OK, once you find it, please show me. Violet, what about you? May I see your sentences?"

Sophia continued to look. She turned her legs to the side of her chair and searched the ground.

"Where could it be?" Sophia whispered to herself.

Then she noticed Sadie contently chewing something on the ground.

"NO!" Sophia shrieked.

She didn't see what it was but she somehow knew. She reached for the paper that was already more than half way in Sadie's mouth. Sadie had a tight grip on it, and Sophia had to pull as hard as she could to pry it out of Sadie's teeth.

The paper ripped in half as Sophia pulled. One

chewed-up, wet piece in Sophia's hand and the other half still in Sadie's mouth.

"Oh no."

"Did you find your journal, Sophia?" Mrs. Robinson asked.

Sophia turned around and showed Mrs. Robinson what was left of the journal.

"Mrs. Robinson, I'm afraid Sadie ate my journal."

Mrs. Robinson let out a loud sigh before speaking.

"And that, boys and girls, is why we don't have dogs in class."

8

PRESENTING LOGAN

Mrs. Robinson had stayed up most of the night working on a math lesson regarding shapes. Now, Mrs. Robinson had prepared many lesson plans on shapes in her 39 years of teaching, but this one was different. She intended to share a video with the kids, and she even made a slideshow. Mrs. Robinson was very proud of herself for using all the technology at her disposal, and she was eager to share the plan with her students in the morning.

The next day, Mrs. Robinson announced her math plan to the class.

"Today's math lesson is going to be all about shapes because guess what, boys and girls: shapes are everywhere. Shapes are all around us all the time. Shapes can even hide inside of other shapes, and they can be where you least expect them."

"There are shapes hiding right now? Are you for real?" Jake asked.

"Let's remember to raise our hands, boys and girls. But yes, Jake, there are shapes hiding all around us. We just have to look for them."

"I can see a shape. It's right there!" Violet yelled.

"That's wonderful, Violet, and do you know what the shape is?"

"It's a ball," Violet answered proudly.

"A ball is not a shape dear, but does anyone know what shape a ball is?" Mrs. Robinson asked.

"It's round."

"It's a ball-ity-ball."

"It's a circle of course."

"Did someone say ball-ity-ball? That's not even a shape."

"Circle!"

"The answer is circle!"

"I heard a couple of you say circle and that is correct. I want everyone to mute their microphones now so I can begin our lesson," Mrs. Robinson instructed.

Mrs. Robinson leaned her face closer to her computer. The children could no longer see her entire face but instead just her eyes, which her glasses magnified.

"Where is it now? How do I do this? Let me see," Mrs. Robinson murmured to herself.

"Here we go," she announced.

"Are we going somewhere?" Susie asked.

"Well, we are actually going inside my computer. You see I am going to present something to you on my screen, so I need everyone to sit up straight, have their listening ears ready and their eyes on the computer."

"We are going inside your computer. Cool!" said Nate.

"Please, everyone, make sure your microphones are muted and watch the screen. Here we go."

Mrs. Robinson fiddled with her computer some more. As she worked, the kids eagerly waited.

"For some reason it is not working. The option to present went away. I don't know what happened," Mrs. Robinson said.

Then she saw it: Logan was presenting.

Mrs. Robinson frantically looked up at the rest of her screen. What she saw was rows of pictures from Logan's computer. It was an assortment of selfies, some from a distance and a handful of what looked like zoomed-in facial features. She could make out a nose in some, an eye, and even an ear in one. All of them of blond-haired, blue-eyed Logan.

As he continued to scroll, Mrs. Robinson saw that Logan had not only taken dozens and dozens of pictures of himself, but also of his toys. There were rows dedicated to his dinosaur collection, each picture a close-up of each dinosaur he owned.

Then there were rows of his car collection. He had an impressive collection of cars: red ones, blue ones, black ones, even purple and pink ones. Next came the collection of transformers, followed by the collection of building blocks, although they were not as exciting as the dinosaurs and cars.

There must have been hundreds of pictures, and Logan was casually scrolling through them. The kids were no longer muted. Mrs. Robinson's speakers vibrated with yells, laughter, and excitement as Logan continued his presentation.

"Logan! Logan!" Mrs. Robinson tried to get his attention.

"Go back down."

"You have a lot of cars."

"Look at that one!"

"Are those pictures of up your nose?"

"Eww. That is gross."

"I want to present. Can I present next?"

"Go back to the picture of up your nose."

"Logan, I need you to stop presenting so I can get back to my lesson on shapes. Do you hear me, Logan?"

It was no use. The kids continued to comment on the never-ending rows of pictures Logan was scrolling through. Logan was feeling more confident now and giving captions to go with the various pictures. The kids loved every minute of it. There was only one thing for Mrs. Robinson to do.

"Logan! Logan! Can you hear me, Logan? I want you to scroll back to those pictures of your building blocks."

"The building blocks?" he asked.

"Yes, the building blocks. And while he does that, I need everyone else to mute your microphones."

The kids did as they were told. Logan scrolled through the endless pictures trying to find the building blocks. Mrs. Robinson thought she saw a picture of a horse but she didn't say anything. Then there was a picture of what she thought was a pig, but again she didn't say anything.

Finally Logan got to the section of building block pictures and he waited for further instruction.

"There is a change of plans, everyone," Mrs. Robinson announced.

Mrs. Robinson thought back to all the hard work she had done on her shapes presentation. She thought of all the pictures she had saved and the video she had embedded into her slideshow. She thought of the sleep she'd missed out on as she sat hunched over her desk while Fred slept upstairs. She thought of how things never quite go as planned when it comes to teaching kindergarteners.

"Logan will you please click on the red block?" Mrs. Robinson asked.

"Yeah, you mean this one?"

An image of a faded, red, rectangular wooden block appeared on the screen.

"Yes, that's perfect, Logan. Thank you. For today's

lesson on shapes, I present to you Logan and his never-ending pictures of toys. We are going to go through Logan's toys and find the hidden shapes. Now, who can tell me what shape this one is?"

Mrs. Robinson may not be presenting but she is always thinking.

9

EMILY CHATS

Mrs. Robinson had never been big on technology. She had a computer and a phone, but besides the basic functions, she didn't dive deep into what each could do. This was one of the reasons she was so nervous to take on an e-learning class. The technology scared her, or at least the thought of the technology scared her.

She was actually surprised by how quickly she was picking up all the new apps and features she needed to know to teach her class. It made her feel quite proud. She shared her new knowledge with Fred one night over dinner.

"I really am getting the hang of this online learning and all of these new apps they want me to use."

"That's great to hear, dear. I knew you would get the hang of it," Fred said.

He passed her the big bowl of pasta at the center of their dining room table.

"It is great. I feel quite happy about it, in fact. Turns out, for 62, I still have a couple of things up my sleeve," she said with a smile.

"Why yes you do, dear," Fred said while passing the green beans.

"There is this one feature though that I can't get the kids to stop using. It's this thing called chat. It's kind of like text messaging. The kids love sending messages to each other on it. The problem is they do it while I am teaching. It's becoming a bit of a distraction, to say the least."

"Have you asked them to stop?"

"Of course, I have asked them to stop. Are you mad?"

"And they don't?"

"Well, yes, Fred, that is the problem." Mrs. Robinson firmly forked the green bean in front of her.

"Isn't there some kind of function you can do to turn it off?"

Mrs. Robinson almost answered, but then paused. She tilted her head to the side. Then she tilted her head to the other side. She finally answered.

"If there was a way to make it stop, don't you think I would have discovered it by now?"

"I supposed," Fred answered.

Little did Mrs. Robinson know there was a way to turn the chat off; she just hadn't realized it yet. The students used this to their advantage, especially Emily.

The next day in class, Mrs. Robinson had only just started greeting the students when Emily started chatting.

Emily: bee boo boop bee boo boo

Jake: hi

Violet: helllllloooooooooo

Logan: hiiiiiiiiiiiiiiiiiiiiiiiiiiii

Emily: oooooo uuuuuuu iiiiiiii boooboboiuueroieur

Violet: lkjliljilijlijlj

"No more chatting now. It's time to begin our day," Mrs. Robinson said.

Emily continued with a giggle.

Emily: bbbbbyyyyyyyyyyyybbbbbyyyyyyyyy

"I said no more chatting. Emily, please quit chatting; it's distracting the other students."

Emily didn't respond but she did quit chatting—for the moment.

"My brother ate a worm yesterday," Jake announced with a giggle.

"A worm?" Mrs. Robinson asked.

Echoes of "eww" were heard throughout the class.

"My brother smashed a worm once," Logan added.

"Gross."

"Mean."

"Why did he do that?"

"Eww."

"That's enough, boys and girls. And remember, we raise our hands when we want to speak, otherwise you won't be able to hear each other."

"I heard him just fine. He said his brother smashed a worm," said Violet.

"No, actually Jake said his brother *ate* a worm," Susie corrected her.

"Yes, but then Logan said his brother smashed one," Violet added.

"That's enough, girls. No more talking unless I call on you," said Mrs. Robinson.

Mrs. Robinson turned to erase the whiteboard behind her. Then she searched for her marker. When she found it, she turned to face the class again.

"Does anyone know what day of the week it is? If yesterday was Sunday, what does that make today?" she asked.

The children began shouting the answer.

"Sunday!"

"Friday!"

"Today."

"Monday."

"Sunday!"

"Saturday."

"Let's sing our 'days of the week' song to help us remember."

Mrs. Robinson began to sing:

Sunday, Monday, Tuesday, Wednesday
next comes Thursday and then Friday
last is Saturday, hooray for Saturday
we made it through another week

"Now, can anyone tell me what day it is, if yesterday was Sunday?"

A sea of Mondays was shouted out, with a couple Sundays and Saturdays mixed in.

"Yes, I heard it. Today is Monday. Let me write that on the board now. Say it with me, Monday."

Mrs. Robinson turned to write it on the board. As she was writing, Emily was chatting.

Emily: hiiiiiiiiiiiiii

Violet: heellelellelelooooo

Jake: u hi u

Logan: lkjljiueoruoeuouoiuoslkjl

Emily: hahahhahahahahahha

Jake: uuuuuu rrrrrrrrr hiiiiii

Emily: ????????

Emily: googoogogooogoooo

Emily: MMMMNNNNDDDDDAAAAA

When Mrs. Robinson was done writing "Monday" on the board, she put her black marker down and took a seat in front of the class.

"Now can anyone tell me …"

Mrs. Robinson stopped mid-sentence when she saw what Emily had started.

"We have talked about this before, you guys. No chatting during class. Please stop so we can continue our lesson."

"I thought this was part of our lesson," said Emily.

"Why would you think writing on chat would be part of your lesson, Emily dear?" Mrs. Robinson asked patiently.

"You were writing Monday down and so I thought we should write Monday down too."

"I don't think that is what you guys were doing."

"Yes, it was. See?"

Mrs. Robinson looked closely at the gibberish written on her screen.

"I don't see any Mondays on there."

"Yes, it's there. Look closer," Emily added.

Mrs. Robinson looked closer and there on the last line she saw Emily had tried to write Monday, in her own special way.

"Is that what that is?" Mrs. Robinson asked.

"It sure is: Monday, M-N-D-A, Monday."

"All righty then. Yes, I see that. You were close. Let's not use chat to write our lessons. OK, boys and girls?" Mrs. Robinson said.

"They really do need to find some way to turn that function off," she murmured to herself.

Then she turned to grab her black marker again to continue her lesson.

10

JACOB, THE PERFORMER

Although it was not a big part of the kindergarten curriculum, Mrs. Robinson enjoyed discussing the importance of heathy eating. The daily schedule included snack time, and Mrs. Robinson encouraged her students to make sure their daily snack was a healthy one. She did not want to see candy bars or sugary snacks. Mrs. Robinson knew what sugar did to five-year-olds. She didn't want to be the one to have to deal with the roller coaster ride that comes with eating sugary foods.

"It's time to grab our healthy snack for the day and read a story. Please take the next couple of minutes to grab your snack and some water, and I'll wait here while you do so. We will start our story in three minutes."

Jacob loved snack time because, luckily for Jacob, he got to grab whatever he wanted from the pantry while his parents worked. Jacob loved to snack. It didn't matter what the snack was, he loved to eat. In fact, Jacob loved to eat all day long.

Jacob was the youngest in his family, with three older brothers. All of them were e-learning together, while both his parents were working from home. The house was full of noise and excitement. Jacob was short with black hair and big eyes. His mom liked to joke that his big eyes were the reason for his big appetite.

Jacob rushed down the stairs to the kitchen. He ran past his father in the office. The door was shut but he could hear him speaking on the phone. He ran past his brother Joey who was on a school meeting at the dining room table. He ran to his mother, who was in the kitchen preparing something.

"What are you making?"

"Joey wants an apple. Jason wants some toast. Justin wants a bar. I suppose you came down for something as well?" his mother asked as she was cutting the apple.

"Yes, I need a snack, but I'll get it," Jacob said.

He walked into to the pantry and began riffling about.

"No, no, no, YES!" he said when he found something that looked satisfying.

"What did you find?" His mother asked.

"Oh, nothing," Jacob said sheepishly.

"Let me see it," his mother demanded.

Jacob lowered his shoulders and opened his closed fist to reveal a handful of candy.

"No candy, Jacob. That's not a snack."

"Fine, then get me a snack," Jacob said.

Jacob took off out of the kitchen for the stairs.

"That is not how you talk to your mom, Jacob, or you can get a snack yourself."

"Sorry, Mom. I am on a meeting. Can you bring it up?"

Of course, he knew she would. And before she could answer, he was already up the stairs. He ran past his brother Justin, in his room on a meeting. Jacob stopped in his doorway.

"Whatcha doing?" he asked.

"I am on a meeting. Get out of here," Justin replied.

Justin got up from his desk and slammed the door. Jacob could hear Mrs. Robinson and quickly sat at his desk.

"Does everyone have their snack?" she asked.

Almost the entire class screamed yes, and then Jacob spoke up.

"Not yet. My mom is getting it."

"OK, wonderful. We are going to start our story then. Today we will be reading a book about a bear, a beetle, and a ladybug and their journey together through the forest. It's one of my favorite stories. Make yourselves comfortable, make sure you can see the screen, and we can get started." Mrs. Robison held up the book.

Jacob looked at the door. His mother was still not there.

"MOM! I need my snack," he screamed.

He waited not more than five seconds before he screamed again, this time louder.

"MOM! She is starting the story. I need my snack."

Still nothing. He scooted around in his chair. He looked at the screen. Mrs. Robinson had opened the book now. Jacob looked back at the door. He listened, but all he could hear was Mrs. Robinson. There was no sign of his mother.

"MOM! SNACK!"

He listened. Still nothing. He waited not more than three seconds before he shouted again.

"MOM! Do you hear me? I need my snack! She already started the story."

Justin's bedroom door, which was right next to Jacob's flung open. The sound startled Jacob and he tipped back in his chair to see what was going on.

"Will you be quiet? I am on a meeting in here," Justin shouted.

"I am on a meeting too and I need my snack."

"I am sure she is coming. Quit yelling," Justin replied. Then he couldn't help but yell for his mother too, "MOM, we need our snacks!"

Finally they heard their mother's footsteps up the stairs.

"I'm coming. Give me a minute."

She could hear they were both in meetings.

"Get back to your meetings," she said.

Jacob kept his eyes on his door, waiting. Their mother walked into Justin's room first to drop off his bar. Then she went to Jacob. She placed a bowl down at his desk.

"Here you go," she said.

"An apple? I didn't want an apple."

He looked at the cut-up apple in front of him.

"I also brought you a bar."

His mother placed a granola bar on his desk.

"Now, pay attention to your meeting."

"It's not a meeting; it's a story."

"OK, pay attention to your story and no goofing off."

A smile came over his face. He smiled because goofing off was what Jacob loved to do. He loved to goof off and make people laugh more than anything in the world. His shenanigans usually didn't work on Justin, since he was the oldest and most mature, but they always worked on Joey and Jason. They also worked on his class.

Jacob waited to hear his mother's footsteps down the stairs and then he turned to look at his screen. Mrs. Robinson was still reading. Jacob had no idea what was happening in the story and he didn't care. He looked down at his apple slices and grabbed the biggest one he could find. Then he plopped it into his mouth.

It was crisp and juicy, just the way he liked. He

looked at the pictures of the few students he could see on his screen. They looked bored. Some of them weren't even paying attention. Poor Mrs. Robinson was losing them. Jacob knew the perfect solution.

He threw another slice of apple into his mouth and chewed it for just a moment. He giggled to himself at the thought of what he was about to do. He looked at his bedroom door one last time to make sure no one was watching.

Once the coast was clear, he leaned forward to put his mouth directly in front of his camera. He opened wide for all to see. Then he waited, apple juice and small bits spewing out of his mouth as he laughed. He kept his mouth there—wide open—for what felt like forever, until he finally heard it. Someone had noticed his efforts.

"Eww, what is that?"

"Gross. What are you doing?"

"Is that Jacob?"

"Is that food? What is that?"

The noise caught Mrs. Robinson's attention.

"I need everyone to please mute your mics and pay attention to the story."

Jacob quickly closed his mouth and sat back before Mrs. Robinson notice what he had done.

He couldn't stop laughing. He plopped another

apple slice into his mouth. He rocked from side to side waiting to do his next performance. Mrs. Robinson continued to read the story.

This time he didn't even glance around to see if he was being watched. He leaned forward and opened his mouth again. This time, drool began to drip down his chin and his laughter made pieces of apple fall to the table. He quickly put his hands to his chin to stop the drool. He laughed harder than he's ever laughed before. Then he waited.

He didn't have to wait long.

"Ewww."

"What is that?"

"Ewww."

"Gross."

"Icky."

"Who is doing that?"

"Stop it!"

Mrs. Robinson stopped reading. She glanced at her screen to see what was going on. Jacob still had his mouth open, not realizing she was watching.

"It's Jacob," said Susie.

When he heard his name he sat back in his chair. He tried to look as if nothing had happened, but he couldn't stop giggling. He continued to chew obnoxiously. He sat up straighter in his chair, proud of himself. All the kids were laughing now.

"What is going on, boys and girls?" Mrs. Robinson asked.

She still hadn't seen what Jacob had done.

"Jacob keeps showing us the food in his mouth," Susie tattled.

"Jacob, is this true?" Mrs. Robinson asked.

Instead of answering, Jacob slouched down in his chair. He almost slid off it entirely. Once he was so low, he bent to the ground so he couldn't be seen. He no longer had a smile on his face. Jacob liked being the class performer, but he didn't like Mrs. Robinson to know about it.

"Jacob? Are you there?" she asked again.

Jacob didn't move. Instead he sat there, waiting for Mrs. Robinson to continue reading and his next opportunity to open wide.

11

FOLLOWING ZOE

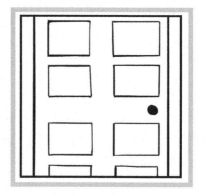

Mrs. Robinson loved Fridays. She loved Fridays for the same reasons everyone loves Fridays: Friday marked the end of a workweek. There was the anticipation and excitement of the coming weekend. People were usually most relaxed on Fridays. The other reason Mrs.

Robinson loved Fridays was because she held a special meeting on Friday for the kids called social time.

Every Friday at 2 p.m., to end their school day, the children in Mrs. Robinson's class would get to come online and just enjoy each other's company. The time was to help foster their relationships with one another. It also allowed Mrs. Robinson a glimpse into the minds and hearts of her students.

Most days, Mrs. Robinson just sat back and listened to the children talk among themselves. They would tell jokes, give updates on their lives, introduce brothers and sisters, share their plans for the weekend, and tell elaborate stories. This social hour had quickly become her favorite part of the week.

This week's social hour started right on time and almost all the kids joined in.

"Hi, everyone. Welcome to social hour. We are just about to get started. It looks like almost everyone is here."

Mrs. Robinson had her head up to her screen as she scanned all the faces in front of her.

"Let's get started. This is your time together. I am going to be here if you need me, but this is your time to do what you please. Enjoy!"

It made Mrs. Robinson feel good to give this time to the kids. She turned down the volume on her computer. She wanted to be able to hear them but she didn't want it to be all she could hear. She got out her stack of lesson plans and began working on next week's lessons. Every once in a while, she would look up at the screen to check on them.

The conversation usually always began with jokes.

"Why did the monkey cross the road?" Emily asked.

The kids talked over each other to answer her.

"To get to the other side."

"Because he wanted to."

"'Cause a dragon was chasing him."

"This is an easy one. Everyone knows this one."

"Why?"

"Nope, none of those are right," Emily giggled.

"I've got one," Logan added.

"No, I've got an even better one," Susie interrupted.

"Hey guys, why was 6 afraid of 7?" Nate asked.

"Everyone knows that one," Logan blurted out.

"Then what is it?" Nate continued.

"Because 7 ate 9," everyone shouted at the same time.

"Do you guys know my sister, Mia?" Violet asked.

Most of the kids shouted "no" as Violet waited for their response.

"Do you want to meet her? She's right here. She's only two. Come here, Mia. Come say hi to the class. Come on," Violet encouraged.

Mia was too smart to go along with it and instead walked out of the room.

"I guess she doesn't want to say hi right now," Violet told her class.

"Do you want to meet my dog, Sadie?" Sophia asked.

"We've met Sadie," Logan blurted out.

"We already know Sadie," Emily added.

"Hey, you guys. Do you want to see my doll-house?" Zoe asked.

"I do," most of the girls replied.

"Sure," Logan added.

"OK, come on. It's in my toy room. It's not far away. It's just in the basement." Zoe picked up her computer and carried it with her.

All the kids could see was a close-up of the bottom of Zoe's chin and the ceiling as she ran around her house.

"What are you doing?" Nate asked.

Zoe wasn't sure who spoke. She looked down at her screen and realized the kids couldn't see where she was going.

"Oh sorry, everyone. Here, is this better?"

She held out the computer in front of her so her face was in the center of the screen. She walked slowly as she talked.

"We are just going down to my basement."

"Where are you now?" Emily asked.

"I am just about to go down my stairs. Want to see?"

"Yes," everyone shouted.

"I know! Do you guys want a tour?"

"Yes," everyone screamed.

"OK, just give me one second to move this around."

She turned her screen to face out and continued down her stairs. When she got to the end, she rounded the corner to enter the living room.

"This is my living room right here." She moved the camera up and down for all to see.

"Don't mind the mess. We don't really clean up a lot nowadays. Those are just all my sister's toys, and these over here are mine."

Zoe tiptoed over piles of dolls, doll clothes, princess figurines, and blocks. There was a deck of cards scattered in one corner of the room. There was a puzzle half done on a table in another corner. Once she cleared the toys, she walked over to the couch where the pillows were stripped off and a tunnel was made.

"This right here is my fort I made all by myself. Well, not entirely all by myself. My dad helped me put the blankets over it."

"Where do you guys sit down? There are no cushions on your couch," Susie asked.

"Well ..." Zoe thought for a minute. "We can't actually sit on the couch right now because of my fort. Good news, though, because this is actually a pirate ship so I can just sail around to where ever I want."

"Can we go inside?" Sophia asked.

"You want to go inside? Yes, of course. Come on, guys."

Zoe breathed heavily into the computer as she pushed her body through the couch cushions and under the blanket. The screen went dark.

"We can't see," Nate yelled.

"It's all dark," Jake added.

"Oh wow, hold on. Let me see if I can do something about that."

Zoe stuck her tongue out as she examined her screen. All the kids could see was her eye, nose, and tongue.

"Hmm. I don't think this is going to work. Sorry,

guys. I'll have to show you another time. Do you still want the rest of the tour?"

"Yes," the kids screamed in unison.

"OK, great. In here is my kitchen. Don't mind the mess," Zoe said as she passed through the kitchen showing the kids the counters, the dishes, the pantry.

"Around this way is our office. My dad works in here," Zoe added.

"Can we see it?" Jacob asked.

"You want to see my dad's office? Umm, sure. Yes, let's go in there. You guys just have to be really quiet, OK, 'cause my dad gets pretty mad if we interrupt him when he is on his important work calls."

Zoe put her finger up to her mouth and slowly turned the doorknob. Her dad's deep voice filled the room.

"Listen. I know what you said but I am going to have to challenge you, Cindy, on that last part you said. I don't think we necessarily need to go down that path."

As her dad talked, Zoe looked at the screen, still with her finger to her lips and a big smile on her face. She scrunched up her nose. Then started to giggle. She moved the camera away from her face so the class could see her dad standing at his desk facing his bookshelf.

"As I said before, I think we will be just fine bypassing all of those steps and getting it done the quick way. Wouldn't you agree?"

Zoe and the rest of her class could no longer stay quiet and laughter sprang out of the computer. Zoe's father turned around to see his daughter standing there with her computer and a big smile.

Without saying a word, he walked over to her and pushed her out of the room. He closed the door behind her.

"That was a close one," Zoe said to her class outside the office door.

"That was my office. Do you guys want to see my room?" Zoe asked.

"Yes," they all shouted again.

"OK, we have to go back upstairs. Oh, and this is my dining room." Zoe moved the camera across her chest so the class could see her dining room.

Dirty dishes, empty water glasses, and crumbs sprinkled the table.

"It's a little messy still from lunch. We had mac and cheese."

Zoe brought the camera in front of her again so the class could see where she was going.

"OK, here we go back upstairs."

When she reached the top of the stairs, she turned

right to go to her room but then stopped.

"Wait—do you want to see my sister's room?" Zoe asked.

"Yes," the kids shouted again.

"OK, right this way, come on. Let's go see." Zoe slowly opened her sister's door.

It wasn't even all the way open when her sister screamed.

"Hey, get out of here, Zoe."

"OK, OK, OK. I was just giving them a tour." Zoe looked at the screen. "Sorry, guys. I guess she doesn't want to be part of our tour. Want to see my parents' room?"

Again the kids answered with an enthusiastic "yes," which excited Zoe to no end.

"Yes, OK, right this way. Their room is the biggest in the house and someday I will have it, I am pretty sure. At least I want it. Wait until you see their bathroom. My parents have a hot tub in their bathroom. Sometimes they let us take a bath in it and it is so fun. It fills up so high. Here, I will show you."

Zoe walked the class across her parents' bedroom. They passed a laundry basket full of clothes, a pile of books on a cluttered nightstand, an unmade bed, and another stack of clothes on the floor next to the bed. Finally she got to the bathroom door.

"Here we are!" she announced.

Zoe opened the door with the camera facing out only to discover her mom sitting on the toilet with her face in one hand and her phone in the other. It took a minute for Zoe to see her. It took another minute for Zoe's mother to look up from her phone to see the sea of faces staring back at her.

"ZOE! WHAT ARE YOU DOING!"

Her mother shrieked with an intensity unlike anything Zoe had ever heard before. At the same time, her mother dropped her phone to the floor and leaned forward in an attempt to cover her exposed body.

"ZOE! Get out of here!"

It was this volume of noise that finally caught the attention of Mrs. Robinson, who had been humming to herself while lesson planning. When she looked up at the screen, she saw what looked like a bathroom floor and then feet running with the camera bouncing with each step. She didn't know what had happened, but she was a smart woman and suspected the worse.

"Oh dear," Mrs. Robinson said to herself.

Mrs. Robinson quickly fumbled with her computer to unmute her microphone and addressed her class.

"That will be enough social time for today, boys and girls. Have a great weekend!"

12

ALEX IS FROZEN

Before the class began their lessons for the day, Mrs. Robinson always liked to start with some fun dance moves. She felt it was important for the kids to exercise their bodies before they exercised their brains. Mrs. Robinson knew how important it was for kids to be active. She also knew kids learn better when they move their bodies and get some of their energy out.

This is why Mrs. Robinson created a special lesson called Let's Move It, and it went something like this.

"OK, boys and girls, you know what time it is. It's Let's Move It time. I want everyone up, out of your seats. I don't care where you are, I just want you to stand up. Come on. Everyone up."

The kids loved this part of their day and eagerly jumped to their feet. Mrs. Robinson started her upbeat music so the class could hear. She adjusted her computer so the kids could see her while she was moving around. The music was still a little low, so she bent over to turn it up.

"There we go. That should do it. Are you ready to move?"

The kids screamed an enthusiastic "yes."

"First things first: let's warm up. Just move with the music. Sway your hips from side to side. Shake those arms and bop that head. We've got to wake our bodies up. Come on, wake up."

Mrs. Robinson shook her arms and wiggled her hips. Then, she stood on one foot while she shook the other one. She rotated feet and did the same. Next, she jumped up and down in place.

It was only her third jump when one of her

beaded earrings dropped to the floor. She bent down to pick it up and set it on her desk.

"Oops, I lost an earring. That's OK. I don't need them."

She quickly took off her other earring so it wouldn't happen again. Then she continued to jump up and down. She was on her second jump when her computer started acting up. She could see her image frozen mid-air. Her eyes were wide open, her hair was hanging in the air, her mouth looked as if she was speaking or about to eat.

"She's frozen!"

"Mrs. Robinson, you are frozen."

"I can't see her. Where did she go?"

The children continued the commentary, since Mrs. Robinson's music could no longer be heard.

The kids slowly stopped jumping and shaking. Then Logan sat down and put his face to the screen. Next, Susie sat down, then Jake, then Emily. It was a domino effect, and in a matter of seconds, all the children were sitting, their faces glued to their screens.

"She's still frozen. Do you see her, you guys?" Logan asked.

"Mrs. Robinson, you are frozen," Susie added.

"Yes, she is frozen. You know what that means. We have no teacher," said Nate.

"What? We have no teacher? What do we do now?" Emily asked.

"Whatever we want, I guess," Jacob answered.

"No teacher, no teacher, we have no teacher," said Nate.

"This is so cool having no teacher. We can do whatever we want," said Logan.

"Yeah, like, we can even pick our noses if we want," Nate added.

"Ick, please do not pick your nose. That's gross," said Violet.

"I already picked my nose," Jake confessed from under his desk.

"There will be no more discussion of noses, boys and girls," said Mrs. Robinson.

"You're back!"

"She's back."

"Quick, everyone hide. She's back."

"Oh no, she's back."

"Yes, I am back. I just had some technical issues, but it looks like everything is running just fine now. Where were we? Oh yes, let's warm up these bodies. Everyone up again, please."

Mrs. Robinson's high-energy song was back on and everyone was jumping about. After just two minutes, Mrs. Robinson called on Alex.

"Alex, you are the person of the day, so that means you get to decide the move of the day. What would you like everyone in the class to do?"

Alex looked down to his feet. His heart began to race. He had never picked the move of the day before. Quickly he replayed in his mind all the other moves picked on previous days. There were so many—jumping jacks, the floss, the shimmy, the sprinkler, the head bang. He didn't know what to pick.

He could feel his face getting warm and he knew that meant it was red. He finally blurted out something he didn't even know existed.

"The rocket?" he said timidly.

"The rocket? I don't think I know that one. Can you show us how it goes?"

No, he could not show them how it went. He didn't even know what it was. What was he supposed to do now? He wished his big sister, Alice, were there. She would know what to do. Maybe he could go get her, he thought. No—no time for that. Everyone was staring at him.

"It goes like this," he began. "First you put your hands above your head like the point of a rocket."

Alex couldn't make eye contact with the screen. He couldn't even keep his head up. Instead he looked down at the floor in front of him. His arms were above his head in the shape of a point. What to do next? His mind went blank, which matched his expression. Then an idea came to him.

"You count!" he blurted out, finally looking at the screen.

"What do you count to?" Mrs. Robinson asked.

"Not to, but down. You count down, like a rocket," he corrected her. "You count down from 10."

"Wonderful, a counting move. I love it. What do you do after you're done counting?"

"You count down from 10 and when you get to zero, you shoot up in the air like a rocket."

"What a great idea, Alex. How about you demonstrate it for us?" Mrs. Robinson suggested.

"Sure, you go like this: 10-9-8-7-6-5-4-3-2-1-0 BLAST OFF!"

Alex shot up in the air like a rocket and mid-air is where he stayed.

"He's frozen."

"Frozen Alex!"

"What happened to him?"

"Looks like he's frozen."

"He froze."

"Funny. Look at him; he is frozen in the air."

"Alex, can you hear me? It looks like you are having some internet problems too. Alex?"

Mrs. Robinson waited for Alex to respond or move, but neither happened.

"Alex, it looks like you are frozen. Can you hear me? Maybe try logging out and logging back in. Alex? Alex, can you hear me?"

Alex didn't know what Mrs. Robinson was talking about because the last thing he heard was "frozen Alex."

No one was moving on his screen. No one was saying a word now.

"Mrs. Robinson? Mrs. Robinson, can you hear me?"

Alex's mother walked into his room.

"What's the matter?" she asked.

"It's frozen," he answered.

"Try logging out and logging back in. It should work. It's working for your sister in her room."

Alex's mother shut down his computer, then turned it back on. She helped him log back in to his class meeting.

"There we go; it looks like it's working just fine."

"Thanks, Mom."

"No problem," she said as she walked back out of his room.

"Alex, I am glad you are back with us. Would you like to try that again for us."

"Sure," he said while sticking his hands above his head.

"10-9-8-7-6-5-4-3-2-1-0 blast off!"

Then up he went again and up he stayed, again.

"He's frozen."

"Frozen Alex."

"Alex is frozen, Alex is frozen."

"Alex, it appears you froze again. Alex can you hear me?" Mrs. Robinson asked.

Alex didn't know what they were talking about, because he couldn't see them. Moments later he was out of the meeting.

"It appears Alex is having technical …" Mrs. Robinson began but no one heard her finish because she, too, was frozen.

"She's frozen," echoed through the class.

"No teacher. You know what that means: it's party time," Nate cheered.

"Party time, everyone," Jacob screamed.

Then Nate froze in place.

"He's frozen."

Then Alex came back on.

"He's back. Alex is back," the class shouted.

Then Violet was frozen.

Then Logan was frozen.

Then Alex was frozen, again.

One by one, all the students in Mrs. Robinson's class became frozen until eventually they were all booted out of their class meeting.

Mrs. Robinson looked at her computer. She tried to figure out what was going on, but she was sure it was the internet connection. Her phone was next to her on the desk and she opened up an internet browser. It was working just fine, which meant it wasn't the internet.

She opened her email and there it was, an email from the school: "There are some technical difficulties that should be cleared up momentarily." She quickly started a new email.

Dear Families,

I am so sorry. It appears that the school is having some technical difficulties. As soon as everything is up and running again, I will let you know and we will resume class. For now, enjoy some time away from your screens. Sorry for the inconvenience, just one of the many joys of e-learning.

Sincerely,

Mrs. Robinson

ABOUT THE AUTHOR

J.H. Kieren loves kids and books, so it only seemed natural that she combine the two. She especially loves her two kids, and she writes about them and their adventures every chance she gets. They inspired a lot of the stories and characters in this book. J.H. Kieren was born and raised in Minnesota, and although she dreams of leaving every winter, she probably won't.

Visit J.H. Kieren at
    www.jhkieren.com

Made in the USA
Monee, IL
01 June 2021

69995293R00069